The Reggae Files

The Reggae Files

By Gordon C

 Hansib Publishing Limited

First published in 1988 by Hansib Publishing Limited,
Tower House, 139/149 Fonthill Road,
London, N4 3HF, England.
Tel: 01-281 1191. Fax: 01-263 9656

Design, typesetting and production by
Hansib Publishing Limited.

Printed in England by Hansib Printing Limited

ISBN 1 870518 03 9

British Library Cataloguing in Publication Data
C. Gordon
The Reggae Files
1. Reggae music. Biographies. Collections
I. Title
784.5'0092'2

The book is dedicated to love

Acknowledgements

The author would like to thank the following
individuals and companies for their assistance:
Gaylene Martin, Margot Bourlet, Peter Lewis,
Claire King, Peter Popovic,
Heidi (Ariola, Vienna), Tommy Noonan,
Llpo Musto, John Warris, Christopher Wright,
Brian Rasic, Hansib Publishing Limited,
People Unite Co-operative, Greensleeves, RAS,
EMI, Island and Virgin Records.

Special thanks to all the interviewed artists
and their managements, Miro, Jan Houghton,
Arif Ali, Rod Leon, Adrian Boot and
Steve Wright. Your positive attitude and support
will always be remembered.

Contents

Foreword

So much has been said and written about reggae music: from its origins in Jamaica, its development through the ska, blue beat and rock steady eras, up to the present day. Rastafarian belief, the back-bone and root of the reggae way of thinking with the former emperor of Ethiopia Haile Selassie at its heart, has also been thoroughly presented and explained in numerous books and publications.

The intention of this book, however, is not to express the author's subjective views and opinions. Its objective is to leave those who create and play reggae music to talk for themselves; to directly express their views of Rastafari, reggae and life, at the same time unveiling something of their personalities.

This approach is intended to be helpful for both readers who know nothing or little about reggae music and those who have a thorough knowledge of it. After reading this book, the former might find themselves listening to reggae for the first time, forming their own opinion of it. On the other hand, for those who are already good friends of reggae, this book is intended to further add to their existing love of reggae music.

This compilation of interviews is the result of my meetings with some of the most prominent exponents of reggae music in London and Vienna. These are the reggae files of the 1980s, this is the reggae way of thinking, or at least, one good part of it.

Gordon C
London, 1988

His foundation is in the holy mountains.

The LORD loveth the gates of Zion more than all the dwellings of Jacob.

Glorious things are spoken of thee,
O city of God. Selah.

I will make mention of Rahab and Babylon to them that know me; behold Philistia and Tyre, with Ethiopia: this man was born there.

And of Zion it shall be said, This and that man were born in her, and the Highest himself shall establish her.

The LORD shall count, when he writeth up the people, that this man was born there. Selah.

The singers as well as the players on instruments shall be there; all my springs are in thee.

Psalm 87
The Bible

Aswad with friend

ASWAD

Top stars of British reggae, "Aswad" were formed in 1975. Their talent made them the first UK reggae band to be signed by a major record company. People from Island Records found it difficult to believe at the time that such young and inexperienced musicians could create and play such good music.

In 1976, the band's first single *Back to Africa* also became their first number one on the reggae charts. The debut album, simply titled *Aswad*, represents one of the pioneer works in terms of British reggae and it contributed significantly to the break-through of the sound created outside Jamaica. In the period to follow, "Aswad" recorded several outstanding singles, such as *Three Babylon*, *It's Not Our Wish*, *Warrior Change* and *Rainbow Culture*. They also provided the musical backing for Burning Spear on his British tour and played on Bob Marley's *Punky Reggae Party* single. The next step was the album *Hulet*, probably the coolest jazz-reggae fusion ever.

By the end of the seventies, "Aswad" compiled their singles and released them in an extended form on the album *Showcase*. Brinsley Forde, the band's singer and *tour de force*, starred in a British movie called *Babylon*, while *Warrior Charge*, voted single of the year by the readers of *Black Music* magazine in 1979, provided the musical backbone to the film's soundtrack.

Late in 1980, "Aswad" signed to CBS and released two fine albums – *New Chapter* and *Not Satisfied*. At the same time, the band was working towards artistic independence; the dub of the *New Chapter* and the *Roots Rocking* single were both released on their own *Simba* label and distributed by Island. "Aswad" temporarily re-signed to Island in 1983 and big commercial success came about that time. The *Live and Direct* album, recorded at the Notting Hill Carnival, climbed high up the British national charts, while "Aswad" found themselves on the front pages of leading music papers, including the *"New Musical Express"*.

"Aswad" more than confirmed their high standing in the eighties with albums *To the Top* and *Distant Thunder* as well as with several outstanding singles such as *Chasing for the Breeze, 56-46 Was My Number, Bubblin'* and *Cool Noh*. In April 1988, "Aswad" had a clear view from the top: *Don't Turn Around* became the most popular single in Britain and the band's first national Number One.

In Arabic, "Aswad" means "black". They are thought of as the first band to play dub live.

BOB MARLEY

Robert Nesta Marley was born on 5 April 1945 in St. Ann's, Jamaica. At the age of 19 he formed "The Wailers" with Bunny Wailer and Peter Tosh. After they had become the most popular band in Jamaica during the late sixties and early seventies, Peter Tosh and Bunny Wailer left in 1973 to pursue successful solo careers. Bob Marley became the leader of "The Wailers" and the vocal trio "I-Trees" and together they gained world recognition for themselves and reggae music, playing the historic concert in the Lyceum, London, in July 1975.

One of the most positive forces in the history of music, Bob Marley used reggae as a platform to sing songs of redemption and liberation for millions. His message and musical mastery will be remembered and remain recorded on such albums as *Survival, Exodus, Natty Dread, Burnin', Live, Rastaman, Vibration, Kaya, Catch a Fire* and *Uprising*. A revolutionary and one of the world's foremost human rights fighters, Bob Marley was, and still is, loved and respected all over the world – from Japan to Germany, Ethiopia to Gabon, Poland to Morocco, Britain to America.

MISTY IN ROOTS

Another top British reggae band, "Misty" came into sharp focus after the release of the *Live at the Counter Eurovision '79.* The album was introduced to the British audience mainly by John Peel, who played it extensively on his Radio One show. *Live at the Counter Eurovision* was acclaimed by Peel and some other radio DJs as one of the best live albums in the history of popular music. This success was followed with three studio albums – *Wise and Foolish*, *Earth* and *Musi-O-Tunya*, the latter being probably the band's best studio work to date. *Musi-O-Tunya* was produced by Michael "Reuben" Campbell, formerly manager and producer of "Aswad". Two songs by "Misty" also deserve a special mention: *Poor and Needy* from the album *Earth* and the single *Own Them, Control Them*.

"Misty" are an excellent band to see live. They are known as a touring band. They have played in Africa (Zambia and Zimbabwe), the whole of Western Europe, as well as in The Soviet Union, Poland and Yugoslavia.

PUMA JONES (BLACK UHURU)

Born in South Carolina and raised in Harlem, Sandra "Puma" Jones holds a Masters degree in Social Work, obtained at Columbia University, New York. On completion of her education, in 1977, she left for Jamaica to put her studies into practice and became involved in the social work projects at Nannyville Community. During that period Puma also participated in African Dance & Drum classes and joined Ras Michael and Sons of Negus, appearing with the band on the legendary 1978 One Love Peace Concert in Kingston, Jamaica.

Legend has it that Puma was heard singing Bob Marley's *Natural Mystic* through an open apartment window; the passer-by was Derrick "Duckie" Simpson who formed "Black Uhuru" in the mid-seventies. He invited Puma to join him and a long time friend Michael Rose, forming the now historic line-up of "Black Uhuru". Propelled by Sly Dunbar and Robbie Shakespeare, "Uhuru" represent one of the most important reggae names of this decade.

In 1980 the band released the legendary *Sinsemillia*

album to great acclaim. *Sinsemillia* was voted reggae album of the year by *Melody Maker* and *Black Echoes*, while the *"NME"* critics placed the LP at number 4 in their list of the year's best albums.

The beautiful vocal harmonies of Michael Rose, Puma and Duckie Simpson, laid on the mighty Sly and Robbie rhythm, proved to be a perfect combination and "Black Uhuru" marked the eighties with several brilliant albums such as *Red*, *Chill Out* and *Anthem*. In 1985 they were voted best reggae band of the year in America and awarded the Grammy Award.

In spite of this success, Michael Rose decided to leave "Black Uhuru" by the end of the same year. He was replaced by Junior Reed and the new line-up released a very good album entitled *Brutal*. A year later, Puma Jones left "Uhuru" to form an all female band.

The present "Black Uhuru" consists of Duckie Simpson, Junior Reed and a lady singer, Funke. The interview with Puma which follows intends to remember "Uhuru" in those terms suggested by the title of their recent album – *Positive* .

DENNIS BOVELL

Dennis Bovell formed Matumbi in the early seventies and the group will be remembered for creating some very good reggae sounds, especially on the albums *Seven Seals* and *Point of View*. On dissolution of "Matumbi", Dennis went solo, at the same time establishing himself as one of the top British reggae producers. He is directly responsible for the memorable single *Silly Games* by Janet Kay and he also produced British "alternatives", the Pop Group and all-female band the "Slits". Dennis recorded several solo albums, sometimes playing all the instruments himself. *I Wah Dub*, *Brain Damage* and *Audio Active* deserve a special mention.

Today, Dennis Bovell is the leader of the Dub Band and the director of LKJ's live and studio performances.

WINSTON REEDY

One of the pioneers of British reggae, Winston Reedy was the singer with the "Cimarons" in the early seventies. After the dissolution of the band he went solo, the most significant steps in his career being the albums *Dim the Light* and *Crossover*. The latter featured several guests, Sly & Robbie among others; he also recorded two outstanding singles – *Superstar* and *Ambition*. *Crossover* was released in 1985 on the "DEP International" label, run by UB40.

MIKEY DREAD

The toaster and the pioneer of Jamaican radio DJing, Mikey Dread recorded several very good albums in the late seventies, such as *World War III* and *Dread at the Controls*. He also collaborated with the "Clash" and produced several tracks on their *Sandinista* album. Early in 1985, Mikey Dread signed to "DEP International" (UB40) and recorded the album *Pave the Way*. He is still DJing all over the world, including Australia, Holland and America.

SLY & ROBBIE

Praised by many music writers as one of the best rhythm sections in the world, Sly Dunbar and Robbie Shakespeare joined forces in the mid-seventies. They set up their own record company "Taxi" and one of the first singles for the label was *Soon Forward* by Gregory Isaacs. Some time later they backed Peter Tosh as members of the "Word Sound and Power" band and toured with him extensively. By the end of the seventies, they were approached by "Black Uhuru", and the collaboration to follow resulted in several historic albums such as *Sinsemillia, Red, Chill Out* and *Anthem*. Sly & Robbie also produced the band.

Musicians of a distinct and powerful sound, Sly Dunbar and Robbie Shakespeare became one of the most wanted "rhythm machines" of the eighties. After they played with nearly everybody in reggae, they set new music standards on the album *Nightclubbing* by Grace Jones. This led them to record with some of the biggest names of the rock world, Mick Jagger and the Rolling Stones, Bob Dylan, Joe Cocker, Ian Dury and Herbie Hancock to name but a few.

In 1985, the "rhythm twins" embarked upon a new era in their artistic career by concentrating on projects of their own. They released the powerful album *Language Barrier*, which featured several guests, including Bob Dylan. In 1987, they climbed high up the British national charts with *Rhythm Killers*, undoubtedly one of the albums of the year. Both records were produced by Bill Laswell & Material.

Sly Dunbar and Robbie Shakespeare have played on so many records that it would be impossible to list them all here. Two recent albums need to be mentioned though: the compilation *Dub Experience* and *Taxi Connection Live in London* which were released in 1986 and 1987 respectively. The 1988 album is called *The Summit*.

LEE PERRY

Lee "Scratch" Perry is the living legend of reggae production. His first encounter with music was back in 1955 when, at the age of 16, he assisted another famous Jamaican pioneer-producer Coxsone Dodd in running the Downbeat sound system. In 1959, Perry was helping Dodd on the audition sessions and he convinced Dodd to sign Toots (of the "Maytals"). Perry also worked on the Toots' first single *6 & 7 Books*.

Gradually, Lee established himself as a producer in his own right. Moreover, he started setting new production standards, followed by other Jamaican masters of the sound. Lee Perry was ahead of his time; only such an eccentric personality could create such an eccentric and "unexpected" sound.

In the late sixties, Perry directly contributed to the growth of "The Wailers". He produced a cluster of "The Wailers" hits, some new versions of which were later re-released – *Lively Up Yourself*, *Kaya*, *Sun is Shining* and *400 Years* among others. The work with Perry and his band, the "Upsetters", directly formed the rhythm section of "The Wailers". Aston "Family Man" and Carlton Barrett of the "Upsetters" joined "The Wailers" at that time to become one of the most exciting bass and drum lines in the history of reggae music. Perry's collaboration with Bob Marley and "The Wailers" also continued in the seventies, and he co-wrote and co-produced several important records – *Punky Reggae Party*, *Blackman Redemption*, *Smile Jamaica* and *Jah Live*.

By that time, the name Lee "Scratch" Perry was firmly established. If it is true to say that Sly and Robbie *played* with nearly everybody in reggae, then it is also true to say that Lee Perry *produced* nearly everybody in Jamaica. Two works deserve special mention: Max Romeo's classic album *War Inna Babylon* and Junior Murvin's all-time reggae hit *Police & Thieves* were both done under Perry's direction. At the same time, he was constantly working on his own projects, influencing Jamaican production with albums such as *Superape*, *The Return of the Superape*, *Roast Fish Collie Weed & Corn Bread*, *Scratch on the Wire* and *Heart of the Ark*.

In the late seventies it was rumoured that Lee had burned down his "Black Ark" studio for personal reasons. It was also said that he had destroyed a good part of his equipment and quitted producing for good.

In 1984 however, "Scratch" was back. He released the album *History Mystery Prophecy* and spent 1985 touring Britain. In 1987, yet another good album by Lee Perry was out. Entitled *Time Boom X De Devil Dead*, this work was co-produced by Adrian Sherwood, a British producer impressed by dub for a long time.

LINTON KWESI JOHNSON

Linton Kwesi Johnson is Britain's foremost reggae poet. The power of his written word has been musically shaped by Dennis Bovell, a British reggae pioneer, and this collaboration has resulted in the high-power connection of poetry and reggae music.

Born in the Jamaican parish of Clarendon, in 1952, Linton arrived in Britain at the age of eleven. He received his education in London, and in 1973 enrolled at the Goldsmith College where he read for a BA degree in Sociology. His political education also took shape during this time and Linton joined the Black Panther Youth League. The Youth League was a department of the Black Panther movement, one of the many black power organisations which flourished in England and north America during the late sixties and early seventies. It was at this time that Linton began writing poetry seriously.

In 1973, Johnson's poem *Voices of the Living and the Dead* was dramatised at the Keskidee Centre in London. The poem was performed with musical backing provided by the band "Rasta Love". This was an embryonic form of the style LKJ was later to develop.

LKJ started recording in 1978 and his debut album *Dread Beat and Blood* was released on the Virgin label. Soon afterwards, Linton signed to Island Records and recorded the lyrical and musical masterpiece *Forces of Victory*. The album was a real break-through for politically aware Linton, a voice of black people in Britain, a voice of the oppressed and dissatisified.

The *Bass Culture* and *LKJ in Dub* albums followed, firmly establishing Linton as one of the foremost reggae artists. He toured Europe extensively with the support of Dennis Bovell's Dub Band. In 1982, LKJ and Dennis produced *Me Cyaan Believe It*, an album by the very talented Jamaican poet Michael Smith.

The insurrections in the British inner cities in the first half of the eighties, as well as the tragic event in London's New Cross, when thirteen partying young blacks died in the unresolved arson, brought Linton back into a studio. The result was the highly political album, *Making History*, released in 1984. At the end of the same year, LKJ and the Dub Band recorded live at the Queen Elizabeth Hall in London. *LKJ Live* on the Rough Trade label, was nominated for the American Grammy Award as one of the best reggae albums of 1985.

Linton Kwesi Johnson has so far published three books of poems. After *Voices of the Living and the Dead*, he published *Dread Beat and Blood* (Bogle L'Ouverture, 1975) and *Inglan is a Bitch* (Race Today, 1980).

The Interviews

ASWAD

Brinsley Forde, Tony Gad, Drummie Zeb

"When you know the power and you have the power, you can use it for either of two things. In everything there is two: there is good and evil. But for a long time what they've done was to tell us that there's black and white struggle. And instead of us looking at the good and evil, we look at black and white and we end up hating each other."

Brinsley Forde, January 1984, London

The Rastafarian belief is based on the verse from the Bible, from Revelation....

Brinsley: You are talking about Revelation 5.5 (recites) "And no one was found to open the book and loose the seven seals...And one of the elders saith unto me, weep not: behold, the Lion of the tribe of Judah, the Root of David, hath prevailed to open the book, and to loose the seven seals thereof."

Is it possible that the Bible talks about some other emperor from the Ethiopian line, Menelik for example, since the whole line is derived from Solomon and Sheeba? Could it be someone else, before Haile Selassie?

Brinsley: Well, you see, it's not for us to question. You see, the things are so simple, yet so complicated, right. It's so simple if you just read what it says, you realise that that was the title *that* man held, which is Lord of Lords and King of Kings, right. Ethiopia was like centuries behind the modern world, since it was never really colonised and subjected to this modernisation. Now, for people who are not educated in that way, most of the British youths and youths in America, or wherever, they are not aware of this. Because most of the black history is eliminated from the books anywhere. So, when people begin to hear this, it sounds very strange to them, you know, and that's why it becomes complicated for people to really grasp it or to understand it. But, I mean, that is the fact, it is the truth. The Twelve Tribes of Israel, as you know, were all scattered and dispersed. Now, it goes on to tell you later that it should be 144,000 of the Twelve Tribes that will go through..."

When angels start to blow?...

Brinsley: ...When the Earth destroys itself. The passage you are saying explains what is happening now. I mean, there is one part that tells you about the white horses that come out and spread this and that on the Earth, there are horses which are bringing wars and rumours of war that have been happening steadily, right, and the next thing to happen is diseases and plagues on the Earth. That's already started in terms of AIDS and it's going to multiply. That's the vision people couldn't understand, and that vision is now. We're beginning to see, to talk about it, you know what I mean? And that vision is what Him was here for. His Majesty Haile Selassie the First of Ethiopia, King of Kings and Lord of Lords who was spoken about in Revelation 5:5 has given us the inspiration...

Drummie: That is why we say Selassie I. Can't question the title he is given. And that title we see as the second coming of Jesus Christ. That's important to each and every one of us.

So Jesus Christ in Rastafari ideology...

Brinsley: Jesus Christ and His Majesty Haile Selassie is one and the same.

Drummie: We feel the same about Jesus Christ as we feel about Haile Selassie. 'Cause he is the second coming of Christ.

Brinsley: And remember, they are from the same root. This is what hasn't been told. Jesus Christ is from the House of Judah, right. So Haile Selassie is related to Jesus Christ right way down to the line of David and Solomon, right way down to the line of Seth, who was the son of Adam and Eve. Seth, Cain and Abel, Adam and Eve. Right to the beginning.

You have played with Bob Marley on his *Punky Reggae Party* single. How did you come together and could you add anything about Bob that has not been said before?

Drummie: I don't think we could add anything that hasn't been said yet about Bob Marley. We know that Bob was a great influence on youths all over the world, no matter what colour, you know, and he made them see that there was a light, right, there was some hope to look for. He opened their eyes to Rastafari and reggae music. His work was not a fun thing or a joke thing, but work which had to be done. The way we came to work with Bob Marley, well, he was here and he needed some musicians to make this record they had an idea of the day before. Him and Upsetter, Scratch (Lee Perry). They just called us...It was a really hot moving experience, you know?

You must have liked it very much.

Drummie: Ya, man, very, very, very much.

Brinsley: Bob is a very strong personality...

Drummie: He's got a power, you just look at him and is like....magical.

Brinsley: Bob said that it's by your works that you live on. The night when that sad news came over, I was sitting with Johnny Osbourne and we sort of left, and went across the road to some brethren yard and they'd been playing Bob Marley. It was like he was there. I mean I watched him on television the other night, he's still here. So....the message of Rastafari is that of love. The heads of Government, they shout for peace, but they are not really dealing with peace.

And this is what Rastafari is here to say. I mean, we could see Rastafari as black youths coming through that line. But, Rastafari is not just for black people, it is for the world, you know. Because Father is our salvation. Beca' simply we know that the Earth is going to destroy itself.

When?

Brinsley: I wouldn't know when. All I know is that we've got to prepare ourselves, because they are going to destroy it. The system that is known now, which we say is the ways of laws of man, that is the destruction. The ways of God are peace and love. Things you feel. I mean, Bob was saying that all the time.

I met you for the first time back in 1980 in Brixton when you played that concert in the "Ritzy" cinema together with Linton Kwesi Johnson. Later, in the dressing room, I said something that you didn't like very much. In all of that after-the-gig excitement I said that you were better than "Steel Pulse", the band that I had considered the best reggae act from Britain. You said that music was not the competition, but rather the way to say some things and survive. Is it still the same, I mean, is there any competition between reggae musicians?

Brinsley: Put it in this way. David Hinds from "Steel Pulse" was down here yesterday. We were together in the cutting room. We are all the same. I mean, we couldn't play about peace and love and have divisions, just because we happen to be "Aswad" and they happen to be "Steel Pulse" or "Misty" or any other band. We are all Rastamen and we're all saying the same message.

Drummie: In our own ways.

Brinsley: As Drummie puts it, in our own ways.

Drummie: We can definitely only speak about ourselves, right. We can't really judge the next man. All we can say is that *we* don't deal with that. We're not in the competition, 'cause music is not competition. Music is love, harmony. When you bring in the competition, you have conflict, you have war...

Brinsley: And then you wouldn't hear about Aswad.

Drummie: I mean, if you have the competition like that, you can't be concentrated on music. We would have stopped ourselves. To be good, you have to go together. Unity is the strength. So whether you're in London...If you know that the next man in Birmingham is going to support you, and a man in Birmingham knows that you gonna support him, yeah...even in that small way, that's the whole hip of change. I mean, if the whole world was like that, just living with their neighbour, it wouldn't be like this now. You have in some parts of the world millions starving, and in the other parts of the world you've got people with so much money

that they don't know what to do with it. You understand? Things are not balanced.

Generally speaking, one small part of today's music can be considered to be an art. On the other hand, you have the strictly music business music which is not art at all. Do you regard your music as the work of art?

Drummie: Definitely.

Brinsley: It will be here for generations and generations. Look, I am not going to put our music in comparison to the Bible but I think anything that gives inspiration comes from God, and if you know it comes from God, it becomes God's work. And you do to the best of your abilities and therefore it's written as a statement that becomes the art. But, in terms of music, what is happening now, I mean overall, is good, yeah, whether it's soul, or whatever kind of music. I mean, what is happening now is what has been *said* on the music. People listen to lyrics, and if they like them, they'll sit down and listen to it again. Lots of artists who are now popular and getting a lot of air-play are either...sexually not what we would agree with...You have that unisex thing, man dressing like woman, woman like man. And remember, music teaches the youth, seen?

Can music change the world? Can it be used as the weapon for the awakening of the mind?

Drummie: That's the most crucial weapon, but it's not been utilised. It's not been used...

Brinsley: Or...it's been used, but it's not been allowed to be heard. Basically, to understand what we are saying, you have to realise that the whole world is fooled by certain people. They've told people about God, right, you have the churches...People believe in God, but tend to go astray from it, because the teachings they've been given are far-fetched, they are not meaningful to how people live today. I don't want to go fully into it, but basically...in the Christmas period, right...we don't believe in Christmas. We know as a fact it doesn't have anything to do with the birth of Christ, but it was set up by the same people who try to fool everyone. They make people get up and say, well, this is 25

December, this is the day of good loving and peace towards men, or what have you, and...they don't stop making arms even on that day! They don't put that money into starvation, or development of people...We could say the Third World, yes, but when you check it, even in America and England you have the people who are suffering in the same sad way, you know what I mean? In ancient Rome, right, they had enough Christian martyrs and they were killing people for even saying "God" or "Jesus Christ". Then, they turn around one day and them say: "All right, we can't fight these people any more. So what do we do? We'll say Jesus Christ as well." They take on the name of Jesus Christ, but they don't take on the gospels, the ways of the teachings of Jesus Christ. They twist them around and feed them to the people. They are not dealing with God, or with the God we feel. (pauses).... This is why lots of people say: "Well, how could God really allow wars and things to go on?" But God doesn't allow these things, God's given man the opportunity to make his own decisions. And man has told himself to be big enough now to make his own laws and to make his own code of morals for people to live by, right? So God had told you that a man is a man, and a woman is a woman, right? But, yet in today's society...equality, you know?

Drummie: You don't know what is what.

Brinsley: In the English system now, I am talking about social security, or whatever, a woman has no longer a need for her man in a role of man. Because all she has to do is to get her money from the Government and to go to the supermarket and get all the things. Her husband doesn't have to go out and hunt anymore. I mean, everything has a balance on the Earth, and as soon as you start upsetting that balance, you get more and more problems. That is why problems escalate, escalate until what?...Until destruction...

One of the basic beliefs of Rastafari is the idea of returning to Africa. I know that there is the Shashamane community in Ethiopia where some of the already repatriated Rastas live. But, when do you think full scale repatriation is going to take place?

Brinsley: Shashamane land is given by Haile Selassie,

man. Africa is the beginning of history, of time. Even men in their ways have proved that the oldest skull-bone fractures and fossils were found in Africa, so we know that life began in Africa.

Drummie: There was civilisation in Africa similar to this a long time ago. Man was flying planes. Centuries ago...

Brinsley: Now, you have America, you have Russia...super-powers. China...Well, they've got their bombs, all of them. Just imagine one day they bomb each other. OK, you've got America destroyed, you've got Russia and China destroyed....

Drummie: And England...

Brinsley: Well, England along with them. What is going to be left? In reality, Africa is going to be the place that is going to have to start running again. Because as it was in the beginning, so shall it be in the end. So, the only people who are going to look to Africa and escape to Africa are the people that really believe in God. And He will give us the sign in time when to leave. All we have to do is to be aware and to watch and perceive the messages when they come. Because it will be mystical. And certain people will just disappear, you know?

So to you, Rastafari is a mystical thing?

Brinsley: You see, people on Earth have always looked for the physical things that they can prove. I mean, you've got Darwin who came up with the theory that says that man came from apes, or whatever. Because, they can't see God. Because they doubt it. They send rockets up there. What do they really send their rockets up there for if not to look for God? So, it is mystical in the sense that there are things that we cannot see, things that you feel, you know, and things which surprise us when they actually happen.

Well, Jamaica is a little island in the Caribbean with about 3 million inhabitants and it has produced reggae which people listen to all over the world.

Brinsley: It's the will of God.

Drummie: That's the natural mystic.

Brinsley: Yes, all of a sudden from this little island of Jamaica you have reggae music. It took the world by storm, it's all over the world. Yet it's not recognised by the major people of the world, but everywhere you go you can listen to it. When God has something to do, seen, we can't question why he does it in that way. He chose the island of Jamaica for his reason. Yes, that's the natural mystic.

BOB MARLEY

"I don't need nobody to come and tell me about this isim and that isim, man. Because...Man!!!"

July 1980, London

Also present was Alan "Skilly" Cole, Bob's long time friend and manager.

Bob, what do you think about playing in a socialist country?

Me? I play in every country, but I don't defend the socialist ideology. I don't believe in it.

You don't believe in socialism?

No.

Why?

Socialism says there's no God. The real socialism, Marx and Lenin socialism. I and I's who'll say Selassi I. If you believe in God and you are Rasta, you cannot be a socialist.

Why not?

Social, I mean, social, socialist, without Marx and Lenin, it's natural living, natural kindness to one another, it's natural God law. Man can't change God's law and call is socialism. Laws of nature must abide in man. All these laws lie there, in nature. So I don't need nobody to come and tell me about this isim or that isim, man. Because...Man!!!

Socialism talks about equal rights ...

Equal rights, socialism no mean equal rights man, because the guys who control the governments, them not equal to the people in the street. There's no way Brezhnev is equal to one of them people in the street!

But some people in socialist countries do believe in God.

Alan "Skilly" Cole: No problem with that. There's no problem there. We are just talking about the socialist policies. We are not talking about the people living there. Don't forget that our Jamaican socialist policies don't have identity with God. You know, you understand?

Bob: First Marx and Lenin send a convoy to overthrow God, right? We are just talking about the Russians invading Ethiopia. Socialism man...we talk about Rastafari and

Rastaisim. I like some people saying Rastafarianism. But isim is fuckery, isim is to divide people them still...

Alan: Ya, man, no isim...

Bob: Them people think...isim, this isim, that isim. Isim mean limited! It put a limit. But if you are Rastafari influenced...all true.

So you would not completely agree with Linton Kwesi Johnson then, since in one of his songs he says "leggo religion"?

Bob: No, man, you cannot fight, there is no struggle when there's no fight for God, man. All of them men fight in vain,

Bob Marley with the former Prime Minister of Jamaica, Michael Manley, left, and Edward Seaga

Bob Marley and the Wailers
Clockwise from Bob Marley: Carly (Carlton Barrett), Tyrone Downie,
Junior Marvin, Earl (Wire) Lindo, Alvin (Seeko) Patterson,
Arton (Family Man) Barrett, Al Anderson

Bob: No, man, you cannot fight, there is no struggle when there's no fight for God, man. All of them men fight in vain, vexation and...pride. You know. Everyone...(pauses)...But, that's I and I, Rastafar I...That's important thing. Because...lot of people suffer and them feel like why do we suffer, and it's system, system who make them suffer, right? At the same time you have Rastafari, so you can guide them through the system not to suffer, you understand? So you know, it's who want what...and from where...Rastafari gives man life. Internal incandle, that's Jah man...Infinite truth keeping in tune with the positive vibration...One positive vibration 'pon the Earth, Rasta...it's the only man who says life ever. Rasta is the only man who say: "Life for ever!"

(long silence)

"The Wailers" were formed in 1964. In the late sixties you left Jamaica and went to America. Was that some kind of disappointment in music...

What?

That period, when you had left for America.

Mother send for American youth, my mother send for me. I've been with my mother. You know? She sent for me.

Did Americans really call you to go to fight in Vietnam?

Almost...

What do you think about what Peter's doing?

Like what?

Like music.

Well, everybody do anyone, you know?

I've read several books about reggae, about you and Rastafari. Some say that you smoke a pound of ganja a week.

Smoke herb must count to quality, you know... (pauses)... The only place you can read about Rasta is in the Bible. Because the Bible is the only truth of Rasta. Some men write about Rasta, but it's distorted. Some people say that Rasta say that Haile Selassie *was* God. All of that type of statements are foolish. That's how some people write it, you know?

Well, I've read something in the music papers saying that you have found a good way to make money, establishing your own label *Tuff Gong*. What do you think about these people? Can they really feel your music?

You see, I never really check people. Nonsense...I check generations. That means that I don't check people, I check generations. This generation get sick bad. Well, some people are in England, some are in Germany, some in Russia...this generation. I never really check people, because what I have, that I have to keep and check on. That's more important than...programme of this people. Because I know a lot of people in the world have been misled. I really don't look at people in the sense of guidance...(pauses)...But you have to know another thing man. I and I get stronger and stronger man. It's been proved. Everywhere we go we have more crowd than we ever had the first time we've been there. People call me for more and more...This cannot stop man, this is something that cannot stop, it's part of life. Cannot stop!

Bob Marley's magnetic force draws his audience into the water of Crystal Palace Bowl, June 1980

In Africa

MISTY IN ROOTS

D. Tyson Tafadzwa,
W. Tyson Poko,
D. Briscoe Tauwanda,
D. Augustine Tendai,
J. Brown Munya,
A.A. Henry Tsungirai,
I. Crossfield Kaziwai,
D. McKay Ngoni

"We know how it is to live in rich man's house, because we live in it. Well, it's true...like a slave is in a rich man's house."

D. McKay Ngoni, April 1985, London

Spiritual reggae is made by spiritual people. How difficult is it to make such reggae in a society of materialism and full rationalism?

Ngoni: Well, you have to have certain strength to overcome [those things] still, you know? Because, all right, spiritual man makes spiritual reggae...but, the roots of reggae is about suffering, reggae is a cry really. It's a sufferer's cry...so therefore all depends on the strength you have to overcome, 'cause some man can overcome, some man will run buttons and do things like that...some will go out there and do craziest things beca' they cannot overcome. But if you have a certain knowledge that all this thing around is a temptation which leads you to destruction really because you get so involved...To overcome these...you know, deep problems, really, you have a chance...of living above these things. But everybody...we all live with it, we all live with these material things around us. Nobody can say that they don't deal with it. Well, I deal with it, you understand? But you have to lift yourself onto a little higher level, where it doesn't...destroy you or make you so possessed to have this or that, better car, video, these things. Because people go out there and thief, to get these things, you understand? And they forget the basic principle of life which is being able to live with one another. They forget about this which is important. That's why turmoil in the world live, beca' people can't *live* with each other, you understand?

When do you think the racial fight is going to stop? Especially between black people and white people. Is this strife going to stop at all?

Ngoni: Well, there is no real racial struggle, may I say that right now, there isn't racial struggle. That is employed to stop people from going a little bit further. It's just an obstacle which they put in our way. All over the world you go, you will find mixed people, mixed races, and different people... Because it's like, once I and I sit here together... for once I and I begin to communicate as man to man, you will see all these differences as non existent. They *don't* really exist. They put those things to obstruct the reaching of a certain... level, as unity amongst men, you understand.

Clarence: Yeah, man. In reality the thing is not between black and white, the thing about a man living with a man goes first, you know. In reality, it is about good and bad. That's what reality is about. Good and bad.

Can you believe that "Aswad" say the same thing? I mean, my question was not the same, but the conclusion was the same.

Ngoni: Yes, because it does not change, that thing. It's the same all the time!

Your first big success was the album *Live at the Counter Eurovision '79*. Do you think that you are better as a live band? In other words, do you think that you have succeeded in adequately transferring the energy of your live performances to your studio works, like *Wise and Foolish* or *Earth*?

Ngoni: Well, yeah, I believe that we are better live, because we've always been the band which performed more live shows. Not like other bands, just really making records and things like that. Where they "fill up", they get that force on their record...we get that force through our live performances. You see, when you have live shows you have that atmosphere, everybody knows that.

My personal view is that on your third studio album *Musi-O-Tunya* you came closest to bringing that live energy to a studio. Especially in songs like *Iration* and *Praises*. Probably *Musi-O-Tunya* is the best studio album you've recorded to date. And production is very good.

Ngoni: Well, you see, that goes like...the more studio work we do, the more we'll get those vibes into the studio music, you understand? You have to check that.

Clarence: If one doesn't progress, one is going backwards.

Listening to the track *Iration* though, I had Bunny Wailer in my mind.

(they laugh with acceptance)

Clarence: That man will tell you better, but if it does sound like Bunny Wailer, I don't think that's deliberate.

Ngoni: It is just the atmosphere, I suppose you can say that. Yes.

Do you see yourself consciously making a commercial single in order to make a big, real breakthrough on the national charts? I mean a good, intentional, commercial single which you would be satisfied with.

Ngoni: Let me say this to you. You never know what's going to be a commercial success. You never know, you just keep your sincerity and out of that sincerity good will come. Isn't it?

Clarence: All right, as Ngoni says. Every man talks about his thing differently, but if a man is doing something that is good, right, there is no need to change, because people must come to that good.

Actually you believe that the audience should follow artists, rather than artists following the audience.

Ngoni: Yes. We believe in what we are doing. Our followers, right...we have a certain, how could I call it...

Clarence: Well, certain cult following.

Ngoni: Yeah, but...we have certain [things] we have to do for them. So we have to live up to what we say. If we are aware of what we believe in, and that is that we shouldn't betray things, there's no reason why we should change. I mean, what is like a man making soul music? Well, let them be! Let them be! You understand? Because we have our following...it could be ten...We played to one man already, you know...So even if there is one man, we are not really worried about that. Figures...you understand? We'll just hold on to our sincerity and if big success comes out of that sincerity, it will be a *good* success. Because directly, we have children, and we want to do what we do for our children, and our children's children. Something that we can grow together with. And that takes the time to build. Commercial success cannot really give us those things, you understand?

Ngoni

Clarence: The other thing is, who makes the music popular, you know? When you check the things which become popular, it is not that people who go out and buy a record decide that music is popular. It is the media who decide to push a thing up to a person, to tell him what is popular. Therefore you have lots of strong artists out there playing music, but because the media does not think that that music is popular, people never get a chance to even hear it. It is the media that shape what people should hear or what people should relate to at any particular time. Just like the people who made reggae music popular in the world. They were not foolish artists, the artists, like Burning Spear and "Culture", they were the back-bone to roots of reggae music. And they are the people who are not going to benefit very much from reggae music. I mean, financially and commercially. A lot of people from there that become number one on the reggae charts aren't going to make from it, but others are going to make out of it. Well, then, that stands true for all the black music, from blues, jazz, soul...We are *us* to take that shape. There're certain ways we've learned from that, you know. For example, take the "Last Poets"...I don't know how much you know about the "Last Poets", but for years they were the only American group that was dealing with the roots music. Telling black Americans about their African inheritance and slavery and things like that, right? They didn't make any money from it. The music was too advanced. And now the American media come up with it again and call it rappin'. And that's what the "Last Poets" were doing years before. You know what I mean, years and years before, like from the sixties. And now they come back with the same thing, they shape it, but they don't talk about Africa and people, they are talking about big "Zodiac" car and all the fantasies of the world.

Are those the reasons why you have established your own co-operative label, "People Unite"?

Ngoni: It's the co-operative to work together. To co-operate socially.

Clarence: To have social awareness of living together and helping each other. You see, I was not born in England. I was born in the Caribbean where people are used to a basic form of social living. Most people think, all right, we are living in England and things are quite easy. But, in reality it's not so easy, you know? If you look from the outside, it may seem easy, but from the inside, there's a lot of hardship within. You have so many people who are unemployed and unable to do something creative, which is important. So we came together to build for ourself, right, rather than just being used and drove by what's already out deh.

You have played in many different places. In Africa, Zimbabwe, Zambia...you have been in Eastern Europe as well. The response of audiences must vary in different places.

Ngoni: Well, there is a difference, really, because in certain places music relates to people differently, you see. Directly, all right, like in Africa we sing a song the people can relate [to], because they are going through that livity. Like in England, you sing a song and some people really don't check us, because they live totally differently from what we are saying. Yes, you do get a different feedback from people, you know what I mean?

Clarence: Yes there is a difference, yet there are a lot of similarities. One thing I am sure [of], everywhere we've played there've been people who could relate to what we say, through true facts...basic truth. Because...I think suffering is all over the world. I don't think there is a perfect place on the planet Earth right now.

How many shows have you played in Poland?

Clarence: Eight shows. Eight very nice concerts. Response was very good, so we go again. Then we go to Russia. You see, places like Poland, Russia, that's a unique opportunity, because not very many people get a chance to get to play to people, as they would say, "on the other side." I mean people in the West, they would tell us "Look, people from Poland or East Germany are completely different people." The reality is that we are all the people, mankind. And to be able to relate to people of a different way of life and culture, that's very nice and important. Because it's reflecting... own culture. And that's nice, you know.

You were the victims of a racial attack in 1979 in Southall. Could you explain what actually happened?

Ngoni: Oh, Gosh, you see...

Clarence: Well, England is a racist society. What happened to us is not unique because it happens to individual people all the time. The system says there is the middle class, the upper class, the working class and the black class...

Ngoni: (laughing ironically) And they call them the minorities...you know, really, they have to exercise authority over minorities...All right, I am going to tell you this. It is very difficult to convey what actually happened, you understand my brethren? We can't really tell you that, it's very difficult. Certain things you probably wouldn't even believe. Blair Peach teacher was killed...Clarence was in a coma...

So, you will keep the message going?

Ngoni: Yes I, as long as Jah gives I strength to do that, you know.

PUMA JONES Black Uhuru

"The plastic smile can't really work in these times."

July 1984, Vienna

You are American...

Yes...

Well, I would like to know how you decided to go to Jamaica.

Eventually, I flew...(smiles)...I just flew away...

I think that _Anthem_ was a brilliant album. But, I was quite disappointed to see that it was not as high on the British charts as one would expect.

Well, it is difficult for me to judge really how the charts operate in Europe, and in England. Perhaps, you know, we can only hope that in the future there'll be more positive promotion, because everyone who wants to actually make an impression on the charts has to have a certain level of imput when it comes to promotion. You know, I mean the full go-behind of the particular project. And I think that our energies were kind of spread throughout the year, dealing with various other issues which meant that all the focus was not really on releases at the particular time. Most of it was about trying to strengthen our internal affairs.

On the one hand, lyrics of "Black Uhuru" are militantly serious, and on the other, one can clearly feel their optimism. But, on every picture I've seen, you look very serious.

Myself?

Yes, yourself, and Duckie and Michael. I don't remember ever seeing a picture in which you are smiling.

Well, that's our particular outlook. We have our time for funny games, but we really take the music and our involvement in the music industry quite seriously, you know, and for more reasons than just to sing and dance. So, most times we would like one to really...take time and really check us out as to what we're dealing with. Because the plastic smile can't really work in these times. You have to know what you are dealing with.

"Black Uhuru" means the black sound of freedom. In

songs like *Youths of Eglington* and *Carbine* from the *Red* album you sing about "cooling off" the weapons. What is your vision of the way to get that freedom and rights?

Well, you see, the perspective varies from place to place. The context of guns and weapons that we use is mostly related to Jamaica. Guns are the political manipulation in our community and one, you know, is in conflict with the other at all times...And people are wasted in the process... They're using the youths and killing the youths at this moment and that's not something we should participate in.

Tommy Noonan

With Michael Rose

How difficult is it to fight for truths and rights in today's world?

Well, you have to fight the good fight, you know what I mean, and it comes from the heart. That's something you are compelled to do. So...you know that this struggle is difficult. Life in general, life for every individual is not easy. Every individual has a particular struggle.

What do you think about British reggae?

Well, it's from its source. It's from its source and it relates to its environment. It's essential to the people in those areas. So, it has to blossom everywhere and the seeds, they sprinkle about and they just have to grow on every corner.

You like some of these bands?

Well, I have respect for every hard-working band out there that's trying to make a mark on the world.

As a Master of Science, I imagine that you find education very important.

It is important, but education is something that can happen in many practical ways. I think that education should be very practical. At the same time, it should be related to building some foundation, some knowledge base that evolves into something. I mean, times change, and I don't feel that emphasis is on college education any more. I don't know, is it?

Well, some people still find it quite important.

Well, I guess it must be, because it becomes almost basic to...earning... depending on what one's ambitions are.

Where do you find insipration for such strong lyrics as in *What is Life* or *Darkness*?

Oh, Michael writes most of the lyrics. So he has the talent for making the stamp, you know, the impressions, words and melody. I mean we all have our particular talents in that way. Duckie writes for the group as well, and I hope to write in the future.

What is the real picture of unity you sing about in *What is Life*?

Well, it's one God, one Aim and one Destiny. In that process each one has to defend truths and rights so that we can break down the barriers that divide us. The unity is...I mean, it is essential to the goal. Every man must set on his path to that destination.

You are the only female member of the band...

Well, that's good opportunity to learn.

Like what?

To be a woman.

Adrian Boot

Black Uhuru, original line-up, full band

Linton Kwesi Johnson

LINTON KWESI JOHNSON and DENNIS BOVELL

"I think that it would be highly arrogant of me to see my poetry as the voice of the Third World. I would be very presumptuous, I would be assuming too much...Even as the voice of black Britain, I am just one voice amongst many others."

LKJ, July 1984, Vienna

"One day Linton came to my studio singing: 'The SPG they are murderers, murderers...' I said: 'Look, I am not putting my name under anything like that!' 'You just make fucking music right and don't worry.' Linton replied, 'It's not me who say that, it's the people. Listen (sings): Everywhere I go I can hear *people* say, the SPG they are murderers, murderers...'"

Dennis Bovell on making
Linton's *Bass Culture* album

What do you think has changed in British society after the insurrections and riots in inner city constituencies?

LKJ: I don't think anything has changed significantly, only to say that those sections of the black community that were suffering from saturation policing are not being saturated any more. We now have a measure of our own strength, what we can do, and the establishment, those who are in power in society, have to take notice of us. So, you will find that both leading parties try to win the black vote. The black vote can decide which party wins, either the Labour Party or the Conservatives. The other development is that there's been a concerted effort on the part of the establishment to nurture the development of our black middle class. So at the moment we are witnessing a kind of upsurgence of the black middle class.

I hope you won't get angry with this question. In one of your interviews earlier on you said that the lyrics of "Aswad" do not deal with reality too much.

Well, I think there is some confusion here. "Aswad" are a band that I liked ever since they came on the scene. What I am against is the escapist aspect of Rastafarianism. I mean, I have been given a reputation of being an anti-Rasta by pop papers. That is not true, I am just anti-negative aspect of it. Whether "Aswad" are Rastas or not doesn't prevent me liking their music.

As far as I know, your influences were Jamaican Rasta influences. You've been influenced by I Roy for example.

It's the true folk culture. What they do is the modern

Adrian Boot

Dennis Bovell in the street

SELF DEFENCE
IS NO OFFENCE
FREE
DARCUS
HOWE

development of Jamaican folk culture. And...I am also influenced by Rasta, you know? Because I remember the particular stage of my development...I took some of the inspiration from Rasta oriented songs. Because even though they have mythological aspect in them, they were very beautiful as works of art, you know.

Dennis, you've been working with a really wide range of musicians, including some white musicians, like the "Pop Group". Is it easy for you to produce a band which doesn't play reggae?

Dennis: What do you mean? What? One thing is as easy as another. I don't know what is easier. I mean, you have a project to produce, you go into it. It could be easy, it could be hard. All that makes it easier depends on a studio, if you've got a good engineer working with you or if the group is exchanging ideas getting things on tape, and so on...

Linton, apart from your career as a poet and a recording artist, you are very well known as a historian of the development of reggae music.

LKJ: I think that at the present time, the music has come full circle. At one time reggae musicians in England were largly influenced by what was happening in Jamaica. Now reggae musicians in Jamaica are being influenced by what is happening in England, right. Bands like "Aswad" and "Steel Pulse" go to play the "Reggae Sunsplash" festival in Jamaica...And some time ago the British based reggae DJ Phillip Levi had the number one tune in the Jamaican hit-parade, called *Mi God, Mi King*. So...I would say at the moment, yes, reggae music in England is on the up, and there is not as many interesting developments in Jamaica at the moment. Only the internationally known bands and artists like "Black Uhuru", Sly & Robbie and Bunny Wailer, people like that, are still making interesting music. By and large, the situation is dominated by the DJs, because the producers find it cheaper to use the old rhythm and to have the D J talk-over. So a great deal of new music is not being created and there is no tremendous amount of new musicians. But, the situation in England is very volatile at the moment.

Dennis: I agree with Linton. Reggae in Britain is widening all the time...branching out!

A very talented young poet Michael Smith was your friend. He was killed in Jamaica. Why did it happen?

LKJ: It happened because that is the nature of Jamaica today. It happened because Jamaica is a very divided society, it's the tribalised society. Over the past decade or so, there was an unprecedented level of barbarism in the society. He was not killed because of any conspiracy, he was stoned to death by some supporters of the Jamaican Labour Party. It could have been the supporters of the People's National Party, it could have been supporters of any political party in Jamaica. They stoned him to death...this is the nature of Jamaican society.

And that is the reason why they shoot at other artists?

LKJ: That's right!

Do you think that your art is going further because you have chosen such a strong medium as reggae?

LKJ: Absolutely. Definitely. Because the poetry itself was very musical and was written within the reggae tradition. And influenced by the exponents of reggae music. It was easier to make it accessible to an audience who might not otherwise be interested in it. So, one tries to get deeply interested in poetry through the music. And I am extremely fortunate in having a set of musicians as talented as the "Dub Band", and a producer as talented as Dennis Bovell, to work with.

What is your solution for the fulfilment of black people's rights in Britain?

Well, we're here to stay. The Asians, the young Asians fighting against fascism came up with the slogan...I can't say it in their language, but in English it was "Come what may, we are here to stay." Blacks in Britain, we have our permanent presence here and we know that we have to build permanent institutions and that the only way to transform our situation is to take part in the struggle for change in Britain. And therefore we are building, and have

Adrian Boot

Dennis Bovell

been building since we've been here, those kinds of institutions and organisations that would take our struggle forward. We don't see ourselves as being separate from the rest of British society. We see ourselves as an integral part of it. It was...It always had that diversity before we came, you know, it was a country of nationalities: the English, the Welsh, the Scottish and the Irish. So we only added to the diversity of the ethnic mix of the society. At the moment, the black working class is the vanguard of working class struggle in Britain. Blacks and miners, these are the only people who are challenging Mrs Thatcher. I think we've made tremendous advances. I believe we are stronger now than we've ever been. Politically and in terms of consciousness.

You are a political activist and popular musician. Could you explain the connection between the two?

Well, some people often sense a contradiction between two roles. One is a matter of commitment and a matter of consciousness, the other is artistic activity. Sometimes the two blend together insofar as I might be inspired by something from my political activity, which I incorporate into my poetry, into my art. But, politics is not work, that's something that I know I have to do. Making records and doing shows and writing poetry, yes, it's artistic activity. I think that the theory which makes the strict division between the politics and art can't stand up to the facts. There are people, there are artists who profess no political affiliations, they are apolitical, they're not concerned with politics at all, and yet they make very sharp political observations about a society in songs, or maybe in movies...And these people claim that they are not political. So...On the other hand, you can be politically a reactionary and make good art, and politically you could be extremely radical and revolutionary and make bad art. T.S. Eliot for instance, I like his work, he was a reactionary, and yet he wrote brilliant poetry. But, when you confuse the two, art and politics, then you become a propagandist, plainly and simply, in the cheapest sense of the word.

Thank you. Before I leave I would just like to ask Dennis

about his favourite producer.

Dennis: I have many. Can't really say. I like different people, I don't know...producer. Maybe someone like Quincy Jones.

LKJ: I just have one last thing. He talked about his favourite producer and one of his favourite producers being Quincy Jones. Well, Dennis is Quincy Jones of reggae music.

Steve Wright

WINSTON REEDY

"If you live today, and you live right, you know you gonna live tomorrow. You don't have to worry about tomorrow. You worry about today. 'Cause you don't know what is going to happen tomorrow. Make sure you do the right thing today and tomorrow will fall into the right. Live good today and you will live tomorrow!"

March 1985, London

Well, I began in a group, as a band singer, you know? I had a band called "The Express". When I left Jamaica, I was not doing music then, I came to England and I realised that I always wanted to do music. So I founded "The Express". It was like the backing business, we used to back a couple of singers, like Eroll Dunkley... Then I branched off with the "Cimarons", still backing Jimmy Cliff and all of them artists which would come over from Jamaica. We used to tour all over England. Then we decided that it was too much backing, you know what I mean? Too much backing. And the "Cimarons" started doing their own thing as the "Cimarons".

In those days there were no reggae bands in England. You were the first...

Well, one of the first. There was also a band called the "Greyhound", then you had the "Cimarons" and "Matumbi".

Dennis Bovell's "Matumbi"?

Yeah. Those were the three majors of the time.

So you can certainly recall the way British reggae developed in the beginning of the seventies.

Well, it was very hard to do reggae at that time, because a lot of bands used to play soul, you know what I mean, and when you start playing reggae, it was like them say:
     "What are you doing man?"
     "Playing reggae man?"
     "You are not going to go anywhere with that music man!"
So ... it was a bit of pressure doing reggae at the time. But we stick to it. We came to the top in that way, you know? 'Cause "The Cimarons" used to come out with different projects all the time.

When "Aswad" started in 1975, the distinction between reggae coming from England and Jamaica could have been clearly made. British reggae was not so..diverse.

Naaah, the sound was soft. Jamaican rhythm was stiff, and

British reggae was soft so most people didn't go for it. But when the artists over here, like "Aswad" and a few others, "Steel Pulse" and, of course, myself...you know what I mean?...started really doing reggae in England, people realised that it can really happen here. But in the beginning...it was really hard.

And so we come to these days. Reggae of the 1980s does not bring such a powerful message like in its golden age, in the second half of the seventies.

The message is not so strong now. I think the reason is that our leader is there, but not really there, in flesh. Bob Marley...he was the one to keep certain things tight messagewise all the time. It is like getting loose without him...It used to be much more serious in the late seventies man. Burning Spear used to really...Bob Marley and others were there to keep the message going. Now is getting kind of loose...

Steve Wright

You are certainly aware of Band Aid projects in England and America. Could it be possible to bring together all the major reggae artists to do the same or similar things?

I thought of that myself too, I think we are kinda slow. I mean, Africa has been starving for a hundred years now, you know what I mean? This Band Aid thing made people say that we should have done the same long time [ago]. I mean, it is difficult, everyone is split all over the world, doing his own thing, but we can still do it, you know?

Well, you mentioned Bob Marley. You know that verse from "Exodus"; "Men and people will fight you down when you see Jah light"?

Yeah. Right.

So...how did you come to it?

I think Jah has come to all men. Black or white...all men. But

it is up to you to know. Because when you feel something, you can recognise it. You know what I mean? You have to recognise it. When I was back in Jamaica in 1976, I was not Rasta then. I was not even thinking about Rasta. But then I went to certain Niyabinghi meetings up in the hills, to play drums and smoke ganja, and I started to take it, to feel it, to feel love man. You get a feeling that you want to do something for people. I said to myself, "I am going to make a new record, do some community work, do something." 'Cause that's what Rasta says: you have to do something for all people.

Even for those who treat you in a bad way?

Of course.

Why?

Maybe you can change them, not all of them, but some of them. Maybe you can change their minds slightly. To stop sticking you and your brother. I think to myself: it is only time before they realise. Even the National Front and somebody like that. If they pass and blood me: (shouts) 'Blood!!!!Black Bway! Blood cloth!!' I say, one day he will learn. I don't feel like stoning him. Only if he physically touches me, that's different, then I have to defend myself. That's why they can't understand about Rasta. You have to defend your brother. In Jamaica, right...when I was a youth, Rasta men and elders would tell me to stay away from them. They are bad. Stay away from Rasta! But them Rasta only teach peace and love at the time and I asked myself how come they preach peace and love and I have to stay away from them? They didn't understand Rasta people. 'Cause Rasta is sometimes like...too aggressive, because the truth is also aggressive.

The truth is aggressive?

Yeah. It is aggressive and very earthful, sometimes. When you speak the truth it sounds earthful. Rasta deals with the truth and reality, with knowing oneself whether one is a white man or a black man. You've got to know your own self. One can be white and know himself and his roots, and he is still white. You can't change that, you must go to your own roots. (pause) Yeah, go back to your roots and know yourself!

How long does it take for a man to know himself?

It can take a hundred years. It can take one second. All you've got to say is: "Yeah, I am going to cut up all the shit and I am going to know myself. I am going to deal with only one subject: Rastafari!" If you go in it and it too hard for you, it means you can't bear it any more. Sometimes you feel you can't bear it anymore. Sometimes you feel crucified. Cyaant cross the road not to be run over.

I think it was a kind of tragedy for Michael Rose to leave "Black Uhuru". Why couldn't that spiritual force and vibration stay together?

Well, I'll tell you something man. Not everything that you read in the book is true. Not every man who looks as a Rasta is really Rasta. There are lots of people in the music business who are preaching one thing, but not living to it. I am not saying that "Black Uhuru" are not what they say they are, I am saying that there are lots of people in the business who only make the material things and fulfil their contracts. And what they sing on their records...you know what I mean?...like...money or drugs.

Drugs? You don't mean ganja, you mean...

No, ganja's not drugs. I mean like sniffing and drinking and...that's drugs. It gives you hallucinations. Some people fall down on stage, they vomit on stage, they are shit man. That is not reggae music. Reggae music is a natural thing. It is. It is a natural thing.

Do you really think that "Black Uhuru" are like that?

I didn't say that. I say that there are lots of people in the music business who are too materialised in certain ways. They don't put their music first or their culture first. They put something else first, like money, or drugs, or girls, or whatever. That's what I've told you about Bob Marley. Whenever he would come out with a record, it would be always A1. A1. He put his music first, 'cause at the end of the day what you are saying to the children is most important, no matter what kind of song you sing. If you sing a love song, you have to deal with something positive, because everyone's got love.

As a lover's rocker you seem to know that well. You seem to be a loving person.

Sometimes. But it was up to me alone. Ninety percent of my songs are like that and people seem to go for it. Lovers. It is up to me to make that kind of music as that's the way I feel. I feel that way whether singing Jah music or not.

What do you personally consider as your biggest success?

Well, when I went solo, after the "Cimarons", I started to improve my music. I think that the most successful thing for me up to now was the record called *Dim the Lights*, that has really opened up a lot of people's ears to Winston Reedy music. Also my first solo record *Daughter of Zion*. Now I have the *Crossover* album out on DEP [International], and I think that people only now notice that I am an original, long-time man.

So, in the end, can I understand that you feel sorry about what has happened to "Black Uhuru?"

Yes, man, I am very sad about "Black Uhuru", Marley, Gregory...

What happened to Gregory?

(Pause)....Nothing happened, but...he's gone...

Soft?

Yeah. He's done a lot anyway, you cyaant really stick him. (pause) Bunny. Bunny is the man who can take the front line. He is the one.

● **Some time after this interview had been given, Gregory Isaacs unfortunately spent a period in prison. Some time after his release, Isaacs made a few brilliant recordings – albums *Private Beach Party* and *Don't Bother Me,* as well as the single *Rumours*.**

Rian Rasic

MIKEY DREAD

"Once I am interested in music and I can communicate on that level, that is all I want. I don't care the colour, I don't care where you come from. Communication is what I deal with. I love that. That's why I've worked with the "Clash" and them guys. If I was just on my own in reggae, a lot of things I wouldn't be aware of."

February 1985, London

When I was a youth there were concerts in my own parish, which is Portland in Jamaica. I was usually the M.C. for those things. It went on and on and on, until I went to Kingston...

What was the time?

'Bout '69 to '72. Then I went to a college, yeah, Kingston, the centre, the city...So I went down and checked the guys at the radio station, they checked me and employed me as a technical operator. I was doing that until 1976 when I started doing my own programme. Gradually improving...But when I started I noticed that one thing was missing from the radio in Jamaica; enough reggae music had not been played.

That's strange. You are actually talking about Jamaican radio not playing reggae music.

Right. Well I felt the problem at the time was that the people who were in charge, had been in charge for years. They were old-fashioned, you know? Jamaican Broadcasting Corporation as former British Broadcasting Corporation, I mean they've got help from the British to set up this radio station, so, normally, they followed what they were told to do from their parents, right, instead of actually catering for the local community. You had lots of British music, British programmes and things like that. It [JBC] was culturally together [with the BBC] in terms of actually grasping the audience. It is a Government station, a national station, right, so they had to be careful about what they did. So, I felt as a young man going there at that time, I had to co-ordinate things in terms of the younger generation of youths who were listening to reggae. Because they'd go to a party and there they'd hear the Heptones, Bob Marley, Dennis Brown and Third World, and on the radio they don't hear them. So I persuaded the people on the radio to go 24 hours, right, as they used to start at 5 o'clock in the morning. I said I would volunteer, because I had just finished my college. I didn't mind staying all night, playing records till 5 o'clock.

From what you have just said, that story about Bob

Marley going to a radio station with a gun...

I've read that, but...

...asking the DJ to play more of his music sounds true.

Well, I don't think he went with a gun, but I think that Bob actually could have gone. Because if they don't play Bob Marley's music, the greatest singer, they show no respect. Even me, I've heard most of Bob Marley's music in England. I think that the problem is that Jamaica is very small, everybody knows everybody, stars do not dress in the expensive garments, stars just look ordinary. So people don't respect them, right. They don't respect them because they think that a star should be like...a pop star.

In the second half of the seventies you recorded a number of quite exciting albums with Sly & Robbie and other famous musicians from Jamaica. After that, you decided to work with the "Clash".

Yeah, well, since 1980. They were in Jamaica in 1981. We worked on the *Sandinista* album, recorded in New York in the "Matrix" studio. We did the *Bankrobber,* you know? The "Clash" was a very conscious group. I love their lyrics and the way they wrote songs. They took a lot of time to perfect, to put the music together. They know they couldn't just make a silly song and go...bam...number one. They were actually interested in the message, you know? But, no, people who listen to music are not interested in a particular message, they just want to dance and that's it.

Well, quite a few reggae singles today are about sensemilia, *Pass me the scale, Sensi for sale, Under Mi Sensi, Herbsman Hustling...*

Yeah, man, because one man tries, and it works, so everyone writes a song.

Mind you, your recent single *Reggae Hit Shot* was quite commercial.

Well, I think it is sort of commercial. It is just an experiment, right. It is not roots, heavy style...I was in America at the time and that song is just...just a basic observation.

Does that observation indicate the way in which reggae musicians have to make their music in order to live? What do you think of reggae at this moment?

Reggae music is not very active right now. Because what you find is like, these guys in England are trying to say that this time is like, the time of British reggae music. We don't like that. That's a silly view of things, man. So, what they are trying to do now is to look for the big British act and to say that things are not one, you know? And reggae music is coming from Rasta. Rasta is from Jamaica, right? We were the first to start this music. It is our idea, so we don't want them in England to say "This is British reggae and foremost", you know? Because sooner or later they are going to take our own culture from us. And leave [us] with nothing. And then...then what they are trying to do is to set standards for us to follow, and if we don't follow those standards, there's no place for us in the business.

When you say British reggae, who are you referring to? You don't mean "Aswad", you don't mean "Steel Pulse"....

Ya, man, "Aswad", "Steel Pulse", everyone in England who makes reggae music. Bway, you cannot compare no one to Jamaican artists.

Well, lots of British reggae musicians are Rastas.

Yeah, but I mean...all right, for example, supposing that in England they make some fine sweaters, right, and they start exporting them all over the world. So you go to Japan and you buy an English sweater, and after a while them in Japan cut the duplicate of your original style, your original creation, right, and they start marketing it saying "This is the year of this." Well...you must feel upset, because you know you did the original, and they take your stuff and sell it to the next man. You must feel upset because he is going to control the market, he is going to brain-wash the audience and say "This is it now." And yours is the original, man, and he is inferior to you.

What can you say about Jamaican reggae then?

(Immediate answer) Jamaican reggae is the best reggae man! (laughs)

Simple as that?

Yeah man, there is no compromise, no guess work about that. If it was not for us...

I mean at this moment.

This moment and for ever more man! And I am serious, man, I know what I am saying. I mix with all of those guys and I know their capabilities. But there is one thing which is holding back everybody – money. And distribution.

Have you made money?

I don't make much money now. The money I make is like working for a group, like the "Clash". Producing them. If I work for a major company, or produce one of their artists, they provide the unlimited studio time. CBS, MCA and other major companies, they've got money to pay, so it can take a whole year to work on one single. One three minute single, until they get it right. Normal artists can't do that. A guy in reggae music cannot afford to spend so much money on one track. And so much time! Guys make an LP in one day, six hours, they can't afford to pay £45 an hour for studio time. It is difficult. When I worked with the "Clash", that was commercially successful. I had my fee. The deal with "UB40" (DEP International) is not a financially rewarding deal as such, they were not prepared to pay too much money. It's just an opportunity of getting the music distributed on a wider level.

Lee Perry is back. What do you think about what he says? He actually accused Island Records and Chris Blackwell of vampirism. And at the same time he has an LP on the "Mango" label, which I understand is the subsidiary of "Island".

(Explosion of laughter) I was shocked with my brethren. I couldn't believe what I was reading. And he was on the radio with Desmond Dekker, I've recorded that! (Another explosion of laughter). That was like culmination!

As a long time DJ and toaster, you must have your view of the British reggae programmes.

Well, there is a DJ on the radio, I read an interview in which he says, well, Rasta idea died out after Bob Marley's death.

Which DJ was that?

A guy from the Capital radio. But that's not true, believe me. So, he doesn't play Rasta music...Rodigan on the Capital, he does not play Rasta music. He and his friends, like guys from "Greensleeves", "Island", "Fashion", they are friends, man. So his idea is to promote his friend's music first. Like Smiley Culture makes a little gimmicky song about the police and they promote it. They like a little bit of humour definitely. But we are serious, we are not in the humour business. So, the serious music is kept out, the humour music is in. They don't play Bunny Wailer music, Burning Spear, or certain militant tunes.

Well, the majority of sound systems in England play roots, but they don't play "Black Uhuru", Bunny Wailer, or Burning Spear.

Because they are from here man. The DJs, they are from England, they might have left Jamaica when they were six years old, and they don't know what is happening. But we have also got to sell our records to survive. To live. I mean...I can do something else, but...I prefer to keep the fire burning!

SLY DUNBAR

"I don't know, lots of people say that I look like a stable person. I don't know, if I am, you have to come around and tell me. It's just me...I don't change, I don't like it any way different, I am like this all the time."

June 1985, London

Sly, can you say why did Michael Rose leave "Black Uhuru"?

Oh, I think there might be some...like domestic problems between Duckie and himself, I don't know what the problem was. He's decided to leave and go on his own, to go solo...Then again Duckie has found somebody else...

Junior Reed?

Yeah. I think *Brutal* sounds great.

You have played on so many records. Apart from your own recordings and those with Robbie, you have played with many popular artists from the rock world. Did you like all of those songs?

Yeah. I think that I like most songs I've performed on.

What was the feeling to work with Jagger and the "Rolling Stones"?

It was great, you know. Because Mick and us are like good friends. And Keith and Charlie...So, you know, when they asked us to play, it was really...We were glad because I think it was an opportunity to really get lots of people who listen to the "Stones" to listen to us as well. As reggae musicians...Same with Bob Dylan. Those are people we really admire.

How much freedom do you have when you play on someone else's album?

Sometimes they give us freedom. When we worked with Bob Dylan on his albums, he gave us a lot of room to work. Jagger sometimes tells us what he wants. He gives us lots of freedom still, but, you know, he tells us what he wants. Bill Laswell is open to everything, he's got his suggestions, but he always listens to what you've got to play.

Is there still anyone in popular music that you would like to play with? One you haven't played with, but you would like to?

I would like to work with Michael Jackson, Quincy Jones and ....Stevie Wonder. Those are giants...We did some

work with James Brown, but he was not too right. I mean the music was right, it was recorded for "Island", but they didn't like the way he was acting. And you know that song by Cindy Lauper, *"Girls just want to have fun"?* We played that. But I think we haven't got a credit for that.

How did you get to work with "Black Uhuru"?

We were playing the rhythm section for Peter Tosh at the time, but we felt it was time to split because we have a kind of music we want to get towards people. And Peter had his own brand. We were producing "Black Uhuru" at the time and everybody seemed to have loved the sound. We decided that it was better if we continued with a new group.

Your images have appeared on several "Black Uhuru" albums, but I was never sure if you and Robbie were members of any band.

I think we are members of the "Taxi Gang" band and the name ("Taxi") belongs to us. We play with "Black Uhuru" and we tour with everybody we would like to tour with, you know, that we can feel comfortable with. But I really enjoy touring with Dean [Fraser] and Nambo [Robinson].

Can you briefly describe the way you work? I mean in a studio.

When we are recording we always go into the studio and rehearse, to get *that* feel. We go to the studio and set up the atmosphere, groove for the record. Sometimes we get that groove in one go. I mean, everybody's there, sometimes we record the sessions with three or four musicians, and when we get the basic track laid, if it sounds great, we might do a little bit of over-dubbing, not much. When we go to tour, we rehearse for a week or so.

Do you feel different when you perform to a Jamaican audience and to a European audience?

I think that I feel in the same way because whenever I perform, I always try to perform to the best of my abilities, you know. I always perform in the same way everywhere, trying to make people enjoy the concert.

But, you know, in some places in Europe people cannot understand the message.

Music is the universal language for people who don't understand the message. I don't know, to be honest, sometimes it seems to me that they don't know what is going on. They dance to the rhythm, you know, they applaud when you have finished, so...

So, you think that it is the rhythm that is more important in Europe?

I believe that for some people the message is also important, but I think that the rhythm is more important. Because most of the singers from Jamaica sing about what's really going on in Jamaica. But you don't live in Jamaica, so you probably don't know what is going on. But reggae can be anything. People always brand us as revolutionary, like the music with the revolutionary message. All right. But reggae can be anything. Like...*Feel on Baby* by Jagger is reggae, *Oooh, La, La, La* by "Kool and the Gang", Jimmy Cliff's *Reggae Nights*, then there's Wilder's song *Break my Strides*...It can be anything. All right, sometimes, it's just a beat...I think reggae is music for everyone, but not just for the ghetto people alone.

I agree, and I also think that *Feel on Baby* is not a bad song at all. However, are you placing yourself amongst the crap you hear on the radio every day?

No. Like...You see, every day you learn. If you hear something that's like, bad...you say..."Oh it could be better"....but anyway, you don't put it down, you know? Sometimes, for the first time you hear it, it doesn't sound good, but if you keep on hearing it, after a while you start liking it.

Reggae originates from the poorest parts of Kingston. It's a musical substitute for many things people would like to have. How do you feel now when you have lots of money..?

(defensive tone and smile) I am not making lots of money. I just make some money to survive....

Sly & Robbie

...Is it still the same? You still get together with old friends?

Ya, man. We don't feel any way different. Me and Robbie, we sit and talk with everybody.

You have been together for over ten years now. Could you ever imagine the thing was going to develop in the way it actually did?

Ooooooh...Me...I really don't know if we've ever imagined the whole thing going like this. We were not looking for the short basis thing, but [rather] long term, and we have decided to put our whole heart and soul into it. Another thing that worked for us was the help of God. We play music still, but everything was given by the Father, he decides what you are going to do next...But to be a successful person, you have to be hard-working, and you have to treat everyone with a certain amount of respect. Because you as an artist are looking for respect from people, so I think artists should treat people with respect also. But Robbie and myself, we still have a long way to go. We have done so much work that a lot of musicians in Jamaica, or even America, haven't done. And we need to do more. At this moment we probably need to concentrate on our own name, [rather] than playing on someone elses record or producing. We are looking forward to that and we're still looking forward to playing for everyone who would like us to play. But, sometimes there is too much work...(smiles)

You spend most of your time in Jamaica?

Yes.

Sometimes I have an impression that some Jamaican artists being in Jamaica, are not conscious of the impact they make on the audience in the "outer world". I suppose you don't have that problem, since you tour so much. I agree with many others who say that you and Robbie are one of the most exciting rhythm sections in the world.

Ooh...Thank you. When you say that, all we do is just...we work harder. You know, we don't take it for granted. A lot of people would say "Aaaa, here we are..." We've never told ourselves that we were the best. Never one day. It's the people them. Robbie has never said "I am the best bass player". I've never said that I was the best drummer. We just play what we feel. Robbie and myself, we are doing this work for people, letting people be happy with the music. If they are happy, we are happy, but if we make the music and we are happy and people are not, I don't think there is something wrong with the music. I mean, we play music for people, so what we do is...we make it simple. So simple that everyone can understand. We make it simple...

But heavy?

Yes. (smiles)

I like Ini Kamoze. His work is quite refreshing for reggae of the eighties. Do you intentionally decide to support someone as talented as Ini?

Yeah, sometimes...You could play with that person live or produce and play the record. But the thing we want to do next is to work on the "Taxi Gang". We are one unit now. To project that sound...This is the time to make a band, a big band with the horns and take it out to tour. I mean, over the last, let's say ten years, reggae has been vocal...people are getting so...accustomed to listening to vocal reggae.
There's nothing wrong with that, but, like in American music you have King Curtis, you have Herbie Hancock who plays instrumental, you could sit down and listen to Chick Corea, you could listen to George Benson...In reggae there is no instrumental of that type to listen to. The reggae market is lacking that. So I am thinking of getting to work seriously on the instrumental market of reggae. I mean...early on, ska, instrumental...it was popular. It died out. We need to rebuild that instrumental status again. So that's what we are going to work on next.

You must be a happy person.

Yeah, man, all the time. You see, as long as the music is right and as long as I can get the time to think about my music and to play it, I always feel happy. That's it. As long as I can play my music, I feel happy.

In the end, from the sea of reggae records you have worked on, could you choose your three favourites?

Three?...You remember *Double Barrel* by Ansell Collins? That's the first record I played on and it was number one. The second...is from my album *Sly Wicked and Slick*...called *Rasta Fiesta*...(thinks for a long time)...One more left, right?...I think *Shine Eye Gal* by "Black Uhuru" is a great song. I mean, I have a lot of songs that I like, but if you ask me for three...that's it."

Adrian Boot

Sly Dunbar "The Taxi Connection"

Lee "Scratch" Perry – Salvador Dali of Reggae Music

LEE "SCRATCH" PERRY

"I ain't got a gun, all I've got is my atomic tongue. That's my atomic bomb! My tongue heals and cures, my tongue is a sword that cuts back and forth...My mouth can do anything. My mouth protects me, man! People are afraid of my tongue and the only chance they've got is to cut it out. And...that is illegal!"

1 November 1987, London

Well Lee, you shocked people some time ago by saying that you had seen Chris Blackwell, the chief of "Island" Records, drinking the blood of a freshly killed chicken. You understand that lots of people find it difficult to believe this.

Well, if people them think it is a lie, those who have a chance of seeing Chris Blackwell should ask him if that is a lie. Anybody have any chance of seeing Chris Blackwell, ask him if it's true or lie, he will tell people if it's true or lie. Because the paper called him asking if he had any comment, and he didn't have none. Well, why didn't he sue me then?

In a court of law? Well, I don't know.

Well, he could sue me for slander if it was a lie. And why didn't he?

That is difficult to answer. Is there anybody else who saw that?

No, it was me and him alone that was there. It is not one of them things where anybody is. Because...hearing about me, lots of people thought that I was one of them people believing in obeah, you understand, voodooisim, but they slip a different thought when they realise what type of person I am. I play the fool catchwise. I play the fool catchwise to see what them top people are dealing with before I expose them. So, he heard from other people of me and he thought I was in voodoo. He thought I was in it and that if he exposes his secret to me, I would expose mine to him. You understand?

Well, now I understand that you are not dealing with obeah, but on your recent album *Time Boom X De Devil Dead* you say "I am a psychy".

I want people to think that I am really crazy! But there are people who already know that I am not crazy.

Straight and direct, it is very difficult too for me to believe that you are crazy, although some people might think so. You also have a 12 inch single entitled *"I am a*

mad man". **Why such a title?**

Because I have a vision, and this vision that I've got is to tell people to repent. When I tell people in Jamaica to repent, then they say me mad. So, me just compete with what they say, I say me a mad man. Yeah!

But you are not?

I didn't say I am mad, they say I am mad . I am the "Upsetter" and I have to make people aware not to be upset by anyone. So if they say I am mad...then I say, yes, I am a mad man! (clapping) Yeah.

Are you sure all of this with "Island" is not just good propaganda?

It is not propaganda, it is for real. If it is not for real he would sue me for defamation of character. But, I don't think he has the nerve to do it.

From the variety of badges and symbols you wear on the cover of your recent single *Jungle***, I can understand that your message is freedom...**

Definitely!

You have that Cambridge University sweat shirt on, but what I do not understand is why do you have that swastika on your cap. Why a swastika, Lee?

Well, swastika didn't belong to Hitler and it didn't belong to Germany. It was stolen from Ethiopia. It was a peace symbol to keep the power of certain race. But Hitler knew the power and therefore he stole it and turned it into an evil movement. So I take it back and I turn it back to good. Me change it from bad to good again!

I thought that the swastika originates from India, that it was a symbol from Indian mythology.*

* Originally, the swastika (meaning in Sanskrit 'well being or good luck') was an ancient symbol in many cultures.

Is it? But what is the difference between India and Ethiopia?

What is the difference between Africa and India? There is no difference.

Well, there is that geographical difference. India is in Asia, Ethiopia is in Africa.

But there was Africa before India. The jungle first, the whole of Africa was just a jungle. And still is. India is not a jungle as Africa is, Africa is the original jungle. Think about it! So, if it was not the Germans who stole the swastika, well, it must have been the Indian then! I know it must come from Africa originally, from Ethiopia, because everything comes from Ethiopia.

So you definitely think that the swastika originates from Ehtiopia?

Everything! Everything! Good and evil. Bad and good. Everything originates from Africa, good originates from Africa, bad originates from Africa.

Why do you think that evil originates in Africa?

Because Africa is the first world. That's where everybody comes from. The Indian comes from Africa, even though he says he comes from India. But there was no India in the beginning, there was only Africa, one big, massive jungle.

Is it true that you do not like to speak about your past at all?

No, it was too bitter! (laughs)

Well, I would not like to go on asking about your past then, but the reason I asked is that I would like to know why did you burn down your Black Ark studio?

Hear me, whoever burned down this studio, whether it's me or God who burned it down, he burned it for his own reason and I have no comment to make on it! I am glad it happened. Me glad it happened! Because if that hadn't happened I would still be in Jamaica right now.

And this is not a time for you to be there?

No.

Why?

Jamaica too local for my intelligence!

What I am puzzled about is this: at the very same time you were telling all these things about Chris Blackwell to the world, you had the album *History, Mistery, Prophecy* released on the "Mango" label, which is the subsidiary of "Island". Did you know that "Mango" was "Island" also?

Of course!

Why did you release *History, Mistery, Prophecy* for "Island" then?

At the time, while I was in Jamaica, I was financially embarrassed; Chris knew it, because he planned the way for me to be financially embarrassed, so that he could take advantage of me, and that was his plan, right? So I had to take money. I was dependent on mercy of his bribe! I was at his mercy for bribing me, because he was not sending me any statement, nor paying me any royalty, right, and then after the studio collapse, I had no cash. So he said: "He has a fucking good album, good material, I'll go down to Jamaica and do that, that, and that, and get it out..."

So, you had to release *History, Mistery, Prophecy* on "Mango", just because of money?

Yes!

Hearing some of your recent material, I could conclude that you are into human rights very much. It seems that you believe that people today care more about animal than human rights.

Definitely!

Do you see yourself as a human rights fighter?

Definitely. Anything me have to lose for it, I will give up! Me see human rights everywhere. Me'll go under the sea, under the earth and everywhere until we get it, until we get human rights. If me have to face a bullet to get human rights, me'll face it! Freedom of speech, do what you want to do, nobody govern you!

Did you hear some new reggae recently, like this album *Jerusalem* by Alpha Blondy and the "Wailers"?

With the "Wailers"? Me don't want to hear nothing about the "Wailers", nothing at all! Because they are out of the picture.

Out of the picture?

Definitely. My name is cold sweat. It's I who paint them in and it's I who paint them out. Right now I don't want to hear anything about the past and they have the past. I'm a table painter. Sometimes I am merciless. When the "Wailers" were on top with Bob Marley, did they have anything good to say about old crazy Lee "Scratch" Perry? Did they? When the "Wailers" were on top with Bob Marley and Island Records, they didn't have anything to say about old, crazy Lee "Scratch" Perry. Then why should I have to say anything about them now? They are out of the picture.

But you did produce the *Punky Reggae Party* single when they were on top.

Everything!!! After everything they can't even tell you it was nobody but me! None of the "Wailers" play on *Punky Reggae Party*. Not even one of them, my friend. Bob was about to lose one of his feet in Miami when I took the tape there. I gave him a word, there's one good thing I love about Bob, his mind very quick, he catch on very quickly. You have to show him only one time and it happens. That's him, Bob. Whenever he made a mistake, it was not my fault. He might have got greedy after some time, but he is a good guy.

What were Bob's mistakes, as you call them? Where did they come from?

Him never believed in black monarchy. And I don't blame him. He didn't believe in black monarchy and I can't blame him, and I can't defend him.

What type of black monarchy?

Black music. And the King is black and God is black. Even the plastic can prove that to you. The record plastic is black. If you don't believe that the King is black, look at the sun when it casts the shadow. It's black. That's the spirit. The spirit is black. Bob didn't believe in that. He thought his own was white or red...He thought his shadow was red and he never knew it was black.

Well, meeting Bob Marley, I could not imagine that someone could be such a believer, so much into Rastafari and into his music.

A man can fly as high as they want to fly Rastafari, but tell them that me, Lee "Scratch" Perry tell them that if they don't remember the son of God whose name is Jesus Christ, they're all dead.

Do you belong to Twelve Tribes of Israel? I mean to the organisation...

(shouts) Me!!! Twelve who? I have nothing to do with anything like that. I closed the doors on Twelve Tribes!

Why?

Because it's not my chance. I have nothing to do with Twelve Tribes, nothing whatsoever.

Does it mean that you have your own vision of Rastafari?

Yes.

And that is...

I am a lonely soldier. From where I came there is no one. I ain't got no mother, no father, no brother, no sister, no friend. No cousin, no uncle, no auntie, no niece, no nephew. I am alone, I am the wind, the wind of time.

It must be difficult to be so alone.

It isn't. When I feel lonely I go and I talk to trees, I kiss the trees and I kiss the flowers and roses and plants and I have fun. I am a fury. I come from Iceland, the fury kingdom. Ice is my crown and ice is my throne. And fire is my heart. And water is my soul.

So, you live love?

Definitely. Love is number one of the ten commandments. Love that hangs all laws and hangs all the prophets by their tongues.

Is there any musician in Jamaica that you respect?

Boris Gardiner.

***I want to wake up with you* Boris Gardiner?**

Not the song that he sings; his talent is extended to one of genius and I have respect for him. To me, Boris Gardiner is the best music player in the universe. Not to say he is the best singer, but me see him as the best bass player in the universe, the best bass player in the Third World. None can compare with Boris Gardiner! He can read music, he can write music and he can sing music.

Your new album *Time Boom X De Devil Dead* was mixed by Adrian Sherwood. Had you heard of him a long time ago?

Who is Adrian Sherwood? He is one of the past, he is not one of the future and I don't want to hear about him any more! He is finished, totally finished, he is wiped out! He asked me to do him a favour, I didn't ask him to do me any. And I did him a favour because he was suffering. I don't need Adrian Sherwood, he is copying Lee "Scratch" Perry, he is doing what Lee "Scratch" Perry used to do twenty-five years ago. Adrian Sherwood needs Lee "Scratch" Perry, but Lee "Scratch" Perry does not need Adrian Sherwood!

But anyway, do you think he is good?

No, he is no good! I don't like people who copy others. He is a good copy artist, but I like people original! He is not original. Dub comes from Jamaica and me the first man that make dub. So, if he was making something different than dub, then I could say "All right, yes", but he is making what I started to make years ago. He is trying to re-create what I created years ago. He is in competition with me and that is the reason he does not have a chance!

But still, do you sympathise with him?

Not at all, I see him as a pagan, next to a vampire. Bloodsucker. Try to steal other people's birth right. There is nothing good I can say about him because he is living off my music and I am not living off his. Him no have no music! If me stupid enough, he might say he was doing something for me, but what is he doing for me? My music, my rhythm, it's we that set up the pattern in Jamaica, and he is trying to copy and be in competition with us. Should be shot!

So, you have an impression that Sherwood wants to compete?

Him no tell me, but me see!

I heard that you were about to produce Paul McCartney. Why didn't it happen?

He did want me to produce his wife, that was his idea. It was an idea to do an album with Linda. Well, Chris wanted a stake, and now we know that Chris is a vampire, so I did three tracks and then cut it, stopped it. I wanted Chris out of it, and, if he was to get out if it, the album would have been finished a long time ago. He wanted to be my manager and that was a mistake, 'cause no one can manage me! It's impossible to manage me!

Was Linda's material good?

Fucking very good! She really sing the truth, she has a very good sense of humour and I think she is a really good woman. Don't let anybody tell you anything else about her, right?

How do you see your musical future?

My musical future? It's massive, big, wide, large! No competition. I was never walking where another was walking. And if anyone wants to walk the road I am walking, they've got to be careful. 'Cause it's not easy!

There have been so many killings in Jamaica recently. They killed Carlton Barrett from the "Wailers", Peter Tosh...Who are those people who go around and kill?

Well, these people are working with politicians. Artists know the truth, artists and musicians that sing and play about political movement. And politicians send people to kill them, to get rid of them, to stop fucking around with their own business and leave them alone. Well, me sorry for Carlton Barrett, but me no sorry for Peter Tosh. Because, the death Carlton met was a plot, but people like Peter Tosh cannot be trusted.

Why?

What do you mean "why"? They are too fucking boastful and too forceful. The only man to be so forceful is Jesus Christ, the son of God, and Jesus Christ is humble. One has to be humble, right?

In life?

Definitely.

If I were to ask you for your message to the world, what would that message be?

Well, my message to the world is love God and live. 'Cause who ever hates God, he will surely die, sooner or later than they think. And it's the faith which is the alternative, and the conscience that is the guide. So, my message to the world is that every man in the world, human being, kids, baby children and mother, have to have some conscience. And let your conscience be your guide. Because if there is no conscience in one, then they are dying. It is the conscience that can bring people to life and it can bring people out of the grave. Jesus said: "I am the way, I am the light, I am the resurrection, no one cometh to the Father but by me." No one can see God but through Jesus. Jesus holds seven keys, Jesus holds the seven seals and Jesus rules the seven seas. Jesus who rules all the water, Jesus who rules all the earth, breeze, all the trees, all the flowers, all the plants and all the roses. And Jesus who rules all creation! The word-name Jesus is alive for ever. A positive expression of feelings. The one who says there is no Jesus and Jesus is not alive, this and that, the first gun shot he gets in his ras claat, he says: "Jesus Christ!", doesn't he? That's the only time when they remember Jesus Christ, when they are in trouble. When they are not in trouble, they

don't remember Jesus. And another way that you can remember Jesus Christ is when you have a woman, and you love her, and you give her good sweet fucking and she says: "Jesus Christ, Almighty God!" (explosion of laughter) Well, my message to the world is to repent and to make the way for the Lord Jesus Christ for the kingdom of God is at hand. And be prepared. That's it.

Finally, where is the place of Haile Selassie in your vision?

Where I see His Imperial Majesty Emperor Selassie I is in my heart. I am a child of the King and I love my Father. Whether he is alive or dead, I still love him. And if he is dead, he won't be dead for long , he will rise again. I know he can rise any time. Emperor Haile Selassie rings all the bells. He can become invisible and do lots of things. He does not have to live in flesh, so that's why he disappeared from Africa. He is in spirit now and has no problems of flesh. Emperor Haile Selassie never told anybody he was God, but people know he is God. Those who look for help from him, they are free to help themselves. Help yourself and God will help you! Emperor Haile Selassie is seeing, hearing, smelling, tasting and feeling. That's super five. His word is alive and his word cannot die. Emperor Haile Selassie is Almighty God, because his is the Bible. Genesis I to Revelation 22. Amen!

"The third error leading to the assumption that there is nothing to be learned about love lies in the confusion between the initial experience of 'falling' in love, and the permanent state of being in love, or as we might better say, of 'standing' in love." *The Art of Loving*, Erich Fromm

"I'm not just a lovie-dove,
I don't just want to fall in love,
I stand in love, not ever on parole."
Wings with Me, Ini Kamoze

Ini Kamoze

Ziggy Marley